BUTTERFLY SNUFF

Butterfly Snuff

A Poetry Collection

Jarred Corona

DEDICATION

*To my sister Bella, without whose support I likely would have
given up on art and myself long ago.*

Part I

A Little Night Theatre

Jarred Corona

A Little Night Theatre of the Tree

A lanky boy with fragmented eyes
and but the whisper of hair
on his scar-woven legs
swings a long stick as if it were an axe
and the Virginia dogwood he imagines chopping
were the flat-faced cat who gouges his flesh
every Wednesday on his way to school.

A tire hangs from a sturdy branch.
When the boy gets tired, he sits and gently rocks.
His uncle once rocked there, too,
the one who scribbled cartoons on packing boxes.
Though, instead of a swing, his uncle rocked
in the embrace of a noose
a couple of years before the boy was born.

With heavy grunts, the boy attacks the tree once more.
Bark flies. Sticks snap apart.
In an hour, the mother steps outside to collect
the boy and all the broken pieces
he inherited from an uncle he never knew.

The Saxophonist

The human puts a golden hook in his mouth
and kisses it for an hour.

A thin noose stretches from gold to flesh
and loops around the man's neck

while he stares at some wordless language
written on thin shaves of mutilated carcass.

He takes a deep breath and pinches the hook
who, in pain, screams and cries.

A crowd watches, and,
in moments of silence, they clap.

Creation Myth, *after Mathias Svalina*

In the beginning there was a child mining lithium for the lithium-core batteries of Eden's first Apple and his pickaxe struck down and his hands felt pancake-snot sticky and he pulled back and a pale blue light glowed from the thin hole in the gray dirt ground and pulsed with a steady EDM beat.

He swayed to music he couldn't hear.

The hole cracked and spread until the light became a mouth that swallowed the boy right before the universe exploded into a single point and that point was a speck on the boy's lithium blue eyes and his eyes shivered in an imagined arctic cold and then the infinitesimally small universe fell as a tear when the boy thought of the taste of apple cider and it splashed as a magenta-tinted ocean on his clavicle.

The universe on his chest glowed.

He could never bend enough to watch the gyrating pulsars dance around black holes beneath his neck but each step of the ballet trembled through to his sclera and it feather tickled and he laughed and the universe fell from his trembling chest and spread at his feet and the flooding waters rose to his ankles and his shins his waist his stomach eyes he stood in the shallow ocean that was all of creation.

Suns scorched his knees and asteroids fileted his thighs.

The boy thought of his mother with her white apron frown that pulled her forehead like a curtain over her dried-mud eyes and how she raised him with a dog's spiked collar locked around his thin neck with a five pound padlock but yet loved him and squeezed his cheeks and offered him a warm glass of milk every night after he washed the mine-dust from his skin and she ingested the lithium pills that stopped her from garroting her not-quite-dainty throat with a sharp necklace made of the boy's ancient baby teeth.

Upon the thought of milk, the boy grew sleepy.

He slept without warning and fell back into the ocean that was the universe and planets settled into his mined open pores and nebula clouds became his gentle breaths and the drumbeat sung in his intestines became music became art became life and death birth murder and marriage and loss

And the people called him *God*

And his coma was called *Grace*

And his waking was *Rapture.*

Steps to Surreal Enlightenment

I.

Hopscotch into the vanilla void,
feel fabric fires devour your lick-heavy skin as
ribbons that burst like springs from broken toys.

II.

Make love inside dried molasses with maggots
        in your flesh,
kiss the child who blood-bathes for warmth in his
        mother's milk,
and cloud that abyssal sky in stars.

III.

Revolt from all our sacred starts:
God is dead, He killed Himself,
the Big Bang was the bullet in his head, the stars his
        spreading blood.

An Oil Painting of Piss Christ, A Mouse

A fanservice horror manga broke a boys' love panel.
The lines crashed off the margins, and a mouse
escaped the printed pages. An ink bleed
flooded the college dorm room like everclear "water,"
blacking out and staining the sheets as it rose.
The mouse floated, a corpse in a formaldehyde jar.

The six-foot business major stood in the rain, mouth ajar
in the quad when the ink shattered the window panels.
It fell in his open mouth and, in bile of his stomach, rose,
escaped creature swimming in his throat. The mouse
spewed past his lips and dissolved in the water.
The young man's eyes started to bleed.

He went to the Catholic ministry to sanctify his bleed.
His roommate texted a pic of a piss coated Christ in a jar.
The priest cleaned out his eyes with holy water
and handed him a pamphlet on a coming young panel
to guide the heart back to Christ and cheese trap the mouse.
For the first time, he thought of giving his roommate a rose.

His roommate was the kind to think Christ never rose.
The oil painter was meant to be the one to canvas bleed,
the way he quiet scurried, turpentine throated, like a mouse
made of vanishing oil. He kept all his blood in a jar
and used it to paint all those spine-shaking panels.
His roommate was oil whereas he was holy water.

He arrived to a clean room, the painter dripping with water,
shirtless just out the shower, and Christ himself rose.

Anger filled the holy man. If God would a jury impanel
against his saving, they would judge the very nosebleed
that came at the sight. So he yelled about the picture of
        Christ in a jar
and used his crucifix to send the morgue his mouse.

He spent his years checking the corners of his throat for
        the mouse.
The laughing girl married him in front of glittering water.
He wished he'd kept, in basement or closet, his mouse
        in a jar
The mouse never texted. Their friendship was no god.
        It never rose.
Oil paintings appeared on his Google searches. His eyes
        resumed their bleed,
but he no longer read manga. He couldn't risk broken
        panels.

Elsewhere in oil panels, mouse kisses once-crucified mouse
on the holes in his wrists where he bleeds holy water.
The business mouse exchanges stocks for a rose,
        and they go home to their jar.

Cigarette Birthed

Her cigarette butt nails, spilling tar on the stiff hospital
mattress, crinkling, embers lifting down yellow streaks,
press against the vice-grip of her only son.
I watch the cracked snowglobes of her eyes.
A smoke mist on a winter wind whispers,
I really messed up this time.

A nurse places electrodes on her flesh
atop the stretching gray veins.
I look away when they lift up her shirt
and hand her the blue plastic bag.

The Marlboro pack is light and empty,
something near to it at least.
A red zippo lighter bounces around in the cardboard
filled with liquified pain pills.
Soon the bag becomes lighter.

The head nurse shoots pointed words.
No one was supposed to be at the suicidal
woman's side to hold her hand
while the wandering automatons refused
to offer a word of update or affirmation.

The snowglobes shattered and the spilling antifreeze sang,
I do not want to die any longer.
Sitting in my car in the parking lot without her,
I think about the nurse's anger she was not alone, afraid,
          haunted.
I shatter, too, and scream.

Though I am a faggot born to a cigarette,
no smoke escapes my lungs.
The yells do not end until I plug my siren self
with an amaretto sour mixed with expired juice.

My mother's lighter rests in my pocket.
The hospital is too far away to burn.
My blood alcohol fire's blue.

The Last Time I Smoked Weed,
I Entered a Manic Torture

The smoke machine is imaginary in Kentucky,
so the student film set out in the cool spring porch
fills with the smog of two pack takes,
green tea rolled vomit vanishing in angles and mistakes.

The herbal remedy exchanges drink for mint;
menthol breaths held in cheeks spill into eyes
for the teared close-ups, breaking, a love
never to be like the ash the non-smoker drips
onto his pants when he doesn't pay attention to the stick
hanging between his chapped and reciting lips.

He retches on his way home.
That's a wrap.

The footage arrives months later,
and no one ever watches.

The Reds Upon the Shooting, Stabbing, Melting, and Burning of Anastasia Romanov

The shaved cougar has urine-tattooed caviars on its tail,
dipped in the edges of the open air aquariums.
Its kittens had mewed in their death beds, gashes filled with
      finish scales.
A hybodus shark bites the line and bloods the water with
      leptospira bacterium.

Oppenheimer was haunted by equations of such an
      extinction event,
shattering singularity turning the irreligious penitent.

An eleven year old boy refreshes the page.
The spinning of the self-chasing arrow Crunches the
      universe.
With a Bang, the boy resets the stage.
He enters the parameters to watch a new form of ancient
      hurts.

He Hammurabis all the evil and cruel.
He invades and immolates invaders.
He makes nooses from the entrails of fools
and hangs all the traitors.

His mother calls him to dinner,
and, giggling, he bounds away.

Break for Dogs

Take a cab
Take a break
Break it off
Break down
Down with capitalism
Down with the sickness
Sickness in the halls
Sickness of the soul
Soul saved
Soul damned
Damned spot
Damned god
God damn it
God save me
Me the dog
Me in time
Time to go
Time is relative
Relative morality
Relative hanging tree
Tree top kaleidoscope
Tree house flames
Flames on the side of my face
Flames surrounding cock
Cock drunk crying
Cockalorum feigning
Feigning desire
Feigning freedom
Freedom from self
Freedom rings

Butterfly Snuff

Rings of silence
Rings of gold
Gold teeth rotting
Gold plates
Plates tectonic
Plates for serving
Serving my crying corpse
Serving fashion
Fashion icons
Fashion a sword
Sword to polish
Sword to swing
Swing at my sword
Swing in the park
Park on the street
Park for dogs
Dogs for hunting
Dogs with fleas
Fleas
hunting

High School Reunion, Valedictorian

Ink covers rivers of graphitic spills
and I cry at results of my own shaving cuts.

Old cats lap at poppy milk.
The puppies die when chasing mailmen.
The deer I hit with my car hobbles off.

Finish the Hat, said Sondheim.
My fingers test the strength of the branch.

Scissors slice open paper people of padded quick notes.
Kill your darlings.

Gems are a myth.
Computonium.

Holy Automation in South Central Kentucky

In the launch of the rocket, standing
amidst the chopped and sharpened corn stalks,
she stares at the high school junior twink
the quiet status rival, music spiller, team leader,
while the others watch the PVC in the sky.
The twink always tenses in his colorblind viewparty,
nervous for splattering heads and
yard darts.

When they're alone in the Yearbook room,
she fakes a limp and whispers about monsters in the room,
how her face is a plastic mask that melts in her bed.
God is working through her. Soon he'll fall in love.
When his eyes remain on the shorn-haired JROTC
man, his laughter at his straight teases, she warns
the twink of the brimstone hell that awaits.
At a field in Washington, rocketry nationals,
they launch in dead air. Near last position their award.
Best dressed.

He could have warned them to wait, their captain,
scarecrow stage straw spilling off a patch on his pants.
The egg in the pool tube lining would not have hatched.
But he looked at the holy water melted automaton
whose pre-scripted clarinet squalls cried
convert convert convert
and he did not share his
spotted thermals.

She returned to the school as a science teacher

happy with the trap-laid spikes of crops and Jesus,
pulled together all the nebula-eyed curious masses,
and taught them to throw themselves as
darts at the yard.

Oscar Isaac Wore a Hat

and Twitter lost its goddamn mind,
invited us to a party where the celebration

    was attempted arson and the party streamers
    tied Poe Dameron by his ankles to a vapid bird

        whose eyes saw gray, black, and white
          but deemed all gray a vantablack

The cap was blue, the text read "Joe"
and just like Ava, the bots came out to kill

    Machinery, Ex Machina, the thrill of preening
    and proving and showing off your perfect skin

      rebrand the choral ode the trending list and bring
        ruin to our tragic fallen figures of new Thebes

Abel beat Kane, a brother in arms
Annihilation in the fascist nation to fascists and

      to Hamlet's Yorick's yore,
      a resistance pilot on our side

      where slight compromise means cannibalize
        one strike and we try to call out.

Fishbowl

A dog runs, dying under the stings of a cloud of bees.
Please, rags, polish the stars, prays one bee, a child who
watches the sky every evening before bed
and who will now perish after stinging a Pomeranian
that wasn't even a threat in the first place.

The man watching from the sidewalk doesn't help despite
the bug spray he keeps hidden in his throat.
See, he doesn't speak the language of *Trying*.
You know how Dick Cheney shot a man in the face
because the universe stopped trying to be subtle?
The man's like that. He stopped giving a shit when his
          mother
told him she wouldn't kill herself
because she didn't want him to find her body
but then did it anyway, and of course left him to clean the
          mess.

She used to keep men in their fishbowl, the dirty one
where fish only ever swam for a week before drowning.
The mermen would appear at night, then disappear
some other morning, flushed down the toilet.
She kept her pain in sex, and sex in the fishbowl.

Rather than love and kind letters left behind to heal
kids and their dissolving angels,
the mother left her son eyes
designed to look at playgrounds and see
monkey bars as sharp neck bones
pursuing dust and death.

Butterfly Snuff

So the man watches the bees sting the dog,
and his only thought is that the neighbor's yard
looks fake, like it was filled with fishbowl decorations
and the trees were designed to be flooded.

Jarred Corona

Part II
Snuff Sublimate

Jarred Corona

The First Erotic Asphyxiation
of a Vanilla-Bean Man

The first time I drank coffee, black,
I wondered if it weren't sweeter than honey
in its bitter refusal to kiss good   bye,
and its grounds, soaked from the   rain,
linger on the doorstep as if waiting   now
for an invitation to come back in   side,
to sink their fangs into my drying   neck
and draw french vanilla from my jugular.

The Turtle Who Sleeps on His Back

Hostel waters spill over my back.
My first kiss is in New York City,
and he pushes me to my knees.
His dick is prettier than his face.

I am Loveless, cat boy manga,
ears and tail still attached, but there is
no magical boy fighter stealing
my born broken heart in the plot.

When he tries to fuck me,
nothing can enter my uptight barrier
depression. My virginity is meant for romance.
It goes to a stranger six months later.

I do not clean my room for my gentlemen callers.
The mess means most never return.
Phantom ants burrow into my flesh
and feast on my hollowing bones.

My heart belongs to roses and candles,
and I whimper on command.
My heart belongs to movies and weddings,
and I die on my back all the time.

Sequestered Seatrain Slut

You are oyster-ovaried, my dad declared,
a sequestered seatrain slut,
scurrying seamen seeding you,
as if you might make life
from the dead and festering fish
inside your guts,

by which he means I must leave Elysium,
Patroclus, pounce forward beyond my
desecrating adolescent rebellion,
unhammock from the quicksand sink
rest upon my back,
uncork the cocks from my core
for I am lifeless,

by which he means my art is a fretful question
what are you doing with your life
interrobang accentuation,
maggots masticating upon my prostate,
dripping come-cancer out a chastity cage
growing growing growing
rubato squalling
creation death death death,

by which he means
I am lazy.

If I were a furry/I'd be a cat

I stoop not to conquer
my bones sag
and crack
cremate

Phantom spiders itching crawl
between my arms' dermis
they multiply
bite

Milk and honey sob rivulets
from under my skin
sticky sweet
churning

Some hairy acid creature reaches
its thick wrist up my throat
I am pregnant gagging
abortion

Estric heat burns in pelvic dances
mewing to be stabbed through
all consumed in
cock

Sunlight stirs serotonin
cosmic caffeine
eye-popping
stabs

By the time the sun hits
and cosmic rays wake
milk and
honey

I am tired
again

Too Anxious to Lobotomize,
Just Anxious Enough to Disappoint

Fashion a leash of flesh 'round my neck
and bark commands, foot on my back.
Drink in tubs. *Sleep* in laundry.
Left to my devices,
static white noise nap,
failson, I am
become Death.
Help me
breathe.

Thoughts when sitting in a theatre design class at 12:07 on a Monday

                                             Yes, it's my
fault that my veins are of fabric, ab-
sorbent, the kind that sucks optical fluid while Death and I
balk at the static, the
bend of chalk letters around my cold breath.

Now my hands stiffen, invisible plaster, they're
longing to tear out my entrails and turn them to patties and
chow, I'm a meal to my masters, the
kings who have stored me in dark laughless comedy,
sitcoms, a fate I deserve for once daring to breathe in gray
dust from a pulsar I loved with a whimpering cry. With a-
plomb, they sent me to reside in this broadcast TV, and they
brush out a hell where I shred all my bones with my
nails.

                What's it like to make love to a flame, to get
fucked into ashes? What mythical masses pre-
vail? Only smoke, vanishing, like the whispers of names,

'til, like my panic, it passes__

Free Use off of Mt. Hood

The laughs and shouts on the side of the mountain
evanesce into the sprinkling flurry.
My feet are cold.

Somewhere on the ski path above, my family falls
from the lift and foal tumble down with newborn eyes.
I remain at the bottom.

The slick slurry of snow beneath the skis
vomit rumbles through my tarsals and femur.
I stand by the roped off river for hours.

The moonlight sea glitters on the trampled slide.
Emergency snowmobiles speed away.
I watch the crowds off to the middle slope side.

They are dead. They are dead. They are dead.
My skis remain buried in the pile,
and I do not move.

We return to the rental house, bruised and tired.
I message the man who said he wished he had a cock
long enough to stab a man through from ass to mouth.

The winds of the calm and empty murder
mountain whisper outside my room.
I slip beneath the covers

and tell him to beat me purple and orange
and fuck me into a pine tree feln chill.
Good boy. Good boy. Good boy.

Hate Sex with the Atmosphere

The boiling Kentucky air must be proud of itself,
being both a pretentious dick and a little bitch,
a new sort of *Ben & Jerry's* flavor from hell.

I've had bronchitis two months now,
and the air keeps grabbing the back of my hair,
thrusting, deep-throat,
so I reach for my inhaler.
At least the air is pretentious,
droning about how I need adversity to survive,
assuming surviving is on my to-do list.
Pretentious dick is just my type.

Sabre-gray winds pick up pollen
and dunk that shit down my nostrils—
that's the little bitch part.
I once got called a little bitch by
the same teenage dirtbags who called me *Fag*
from the comfort of their daddy-bought yee-yee trucks.
They threw deer piss on my faux-leather seats.
As they laughed through their Bible-page veneers,
they cried, *God.*
When I huff bent over the counter, sucking off the sky,
I moan, *God.*

I wish I were on drugs,
not an inhaler, something harder,
but alas, all I have is
this goddamn air,
slow-fucking me.

Snuff Sublimate

Most people who watch non-consensual-play porn,
fingers bread-kneading focaccia from fissured flesh
as they garlic gasp and gulp, tomato vamping through
       veins,
baking breadless selves into starved gluttony's slave,
do not aspire to Hansel into ovens or to Witch any Gretels.

I am the leftovers of a three-course meal.
Enter my house, said the Wizard.
I shall thrust him into the oven, said the Wolf.
Eat of my dessert, said the Witch.

Saliva slides from roof to tongue in the giant of my dreams.
Leviathan lasciviously licks my truest form,
ingestible ingredients contained in a bag of skin.
His teeth graze over my back and legs.
Olive oil coated, I Olympic dive down his throat,
splash into stomach acids, churning, roiling.

Don't digest me, I plead.
But you are food and shit, said the Giant.
Finally put to use.

I have Kafka'd suicide into snuff sublimate,
a swallowee to be subjected to sluice slime.
Transformation to the taboo takes the knife
off my neck. The garotte goes from gallow gore-potential
to a hypnotic fictionality, a never, a whimper.
I do not crash the car.
I do not take the pills.

You can be bread, says Yeast, rediscovered in my gut,
whispering once again that part of me is alive.

The Worm Question

If I woke a worm,
would you take your stretching feet
and flatten me orgasmic?

You would only pass
as a secret between my
lips, protein boost. Us, melded.

Paradelle on the Man I Ought to Block

Two Kentucky birds migrate north and south.
Two Kentucky birds migrate north and south.
He replaced the wine on my lips with his sober sex.
He replaced the wine on my lips with his sober sex.
The wine on my south Kentucky lips replaced with sex,
and he, two birds sober migrate north.

My gentle fist turns red-green-brown angry at his success.
My gentle fist turns red-green-brown angry at his success.
I run from the caves in the ether.
I run from the caves in the ether.
From the red ether, the brown caves, his fist green
at my gentle success, in turns, angry, I run.

The apple falls from psycho gravity.
The apple falls from psycho gravity.
Ignorance shrouds him from knowing he's the only
        name of three.
Ignorance shrouds him from knowing he's the only
        name of three.
Apple ignorance shrouds the three falls from him knowing.
He's from gravity, name of the only psycho.

Gentle green sex falls psycho on my south brown caves,
apple red lips knowing only his Kentucky name.
He's angry in the north from the shrouds of ignorance.
I run from him, he, the fist with success.
My wine turns sober from the three.
Two birds migrate south and, at the ether, replaced gravity.

The Sort of Tears that Come with Porn

When there's a storyline before the shot
where the tall man bumps his twink
who smiles while coated in cum,
I think of you. I can't replace
the actors with myself or think
on how hot the action is.

I miss him, I'll think, my hand
absentminded on my sex,
and as the tears splinter out,
I finish, and can't remember
the porn at all.

When there isn't a storyline before the shot
where their lips press like fingers
brushed through drowsy hair - once, twice,
then long and lingering - I wonder
how they spend the nights without feeling empty
and cold, a phantom against their mouths,
the sort that begs for remembrance but
refuses to be tamed.

I miss him, I'll think, my hand
slipping a sock over myself
with the duty of a twelve-year-old
taking out the trash as self-love is a task
to return to that time where at least my origami body
was okay with being   .

Amaretto, 1998

When he throatfucks me with saliva strings
spilling over his sweet-tasting balls, my brain quiets.

Amaretto tastes sweetest with a
frothing egg white, seeded, savory, spilling over.

Leaving the theatre, musical done,
a truck spots the bandana on my neck and yells, *Fag!*

I am not a percussionist, yet
they pay me to beat an elephant-printed cajon.

The Grindr couple invites me home
to swallow their cum, back and forth, until my exile.

He viewed me like his shot of bourbon:
when he wants sobriety, he pours me down the drain.

If I'm a poison best avoided,
let me be amaretto frothing with tossed egg white.

April 1st until December 8th

The snow in our lungs powers our walk
across the city and the river to a hotel
hot tub unmanned and unbothered
the chill air swirling as a punishment for standing.
His flat chest beats against my back,
low whispers about what he'll do to me,
fingers loose gripping inside my trunks.
He falls asleep on the ferry.
A child points us out to his mother.

Hiccup rage hurls his Heineken beer
bottle at the wall where it shatters in the kitchen.
Day old socks wipe the watery spills from his eyes.
He barefoot walks to the fractal mess.
The dog outside wags his tail, blond, oblivious
that his hair-kinned master was fired.

When our friend asks about the plastic stool
outside under his window where I snuck in and
out in the morning, he claims
his dealer does drive-by delivery.
Rare are the days we share, because the days
are for his sobriety and writing and regret.
He is embarrassed when he bourbon stumbles to bed,
but I am the cancer he longs for in his lungs when
      he is drunk.
When I wanted to discuss our death,
he tucked me into bed, fucked me in the morning,
and killed the conversation.

I'm an asshole, he warned when we first
spoke of love.

I forgave my first love long ago.
So when does my mirror look less like a shattered bottle
glued together in the back of a closet,
hidden under a *Star Wars* blanket with the love
letters he never could throw away?

Monoamine

He said his cock didn't work because
- alcohol
- antidepressants
- coke
- self-hate

He said he didn't bourbon blow his brains because
- his mother
- brother
- dog
- me

I said I stayed with him at first because
- connections
- loneliness
- affirmation
- if he caught my namesake virus
  and purpled my face-fragile lungs
  writhed me in plastic doll tarp hospitals
  no one would ever call it suicide

We can't talk anymore because
- he wants my legs wrapped around napes
  hair against his ever-bruising back
  while he hurries inside my womb shaved ass
  I'm going to get you pregnant
- I want his lips on mine stunk with drink
  paused live music on the TV
  hurriedly off to his bathroom to piss while I text
  Ninja strike! I love you

- we are both temptation
  adams apples of eden
  our teeth sinking into necks
  gluttonous need for copper sweat
- I love him
  I love him
  I love him
  I love him

I take the generic muzzle medication prescribed by the
portly Catholic who doesn't believe in psychiatric care
and swallow a watery mouthful, *this is the way to health*,
and wonder if he tells himself the same.

And She Traded Her Skin for Robes

There is a disgust that comes with her feet
college quad blackened landing on my blue striped sheets
as she tosses above the covers with the blonde teacher-to-be
both dressed in shorts hers denim other sorority.
The bed is mine, much as anything
can be in a freshman dorm,
as is the anxiety I inherited from my mother that prevents
me from saying
stop.

There are eight of us in the room at least
five have a crush on her
as if something in her ferality and sweat calls
them as mother earth
return return my children and feast
do they say nothing because they are entranced
by the dirt on her feet?
We talk of trivial things: sports, classes,
dumpster diving plans, and life.
I do not wash my sheets, though I long to,
because I am tired and
dying.

There are hints in the photos she summer
posts from the wild
she has taken a cat of ninetails holy
water tempered child
and removed to adam an evish rib
to help her self-flagellation

bleeding flesh in ranting posts catholic beauty is
the only beauty of creation.
I visit the Catholic ministry on campus at
3:33 on a Tuesday morning
to vandalize the sidewalks in pale chalk,
the only way the two of us ever
talk.

There is a suffocating stench of rubber seam
glue filling up my car
cardinal perched atop the red hill she sits
passenger a creature
of neoprene robes all black and white in habit
no dirt on her feet
because her feet are no longer feet at all but
separated chaff from wheat.
She tells me my depressive ideation would disappear
if only I was Catholic.
It is loving, says the creature in my car,
Catechism cutting both our
queerness.

The loving priest she tells me to listen to accuses
puppy fucker
as she gifts razors skin carving torture porn
the passion of the christ
was holy because of ascetic pain *it is holy to suffer*
and for the fare you pay the church will trade bdsm robes.
Give us your skin, she cries.
We sit in my car. *Give us your skin.*

She leaves for Spanish nunneries.
All my former friends bid her a fond
farewell.

Part III
The Midnight Butterfly

Jarred Corona

I am Jealous of Butterflies

because the floors in my apartment are thin
the way only paper houses can be

my neighbors are up 2:43 AM,
hyenas cackling at a shrouded moon
as they're off to a party or back from one—
there's always a party in this tiny town
Their voices leak through the wall
and brook-babble mangled words

because something about the cold

feels like jubilation—
a feeling found only in children and reference books—
how your lungs reject your skin
your dried-apricot tongue stutters

because my tongue is nosy
the way my sisters are

it hears the sobs echoing in my teeth
until I have no enamel no teeth no tongue
just a gun the government shouldn't let me buy

because butterflies know nothing
of wanting to die

The Consequences of Being Colorblind

Velvet turtles carry planets on universe-infested backs,
ramming each other as they play bumper-shells.
In their game of galaxy quakes, strings of destiny mix
into new seductive knots, tying new pinkies and changing
        colors.
Red strings connect romance.

In a different universe, on a different turtle's back,
you tease me about color-dot tests,
and our purple melancholies blend lilac.

Delirious with fever, I once called you a deer prince
and, unquestioningly, you named me a princess.
Your emerald pupils migrated down my spine before
they dared to make eye contact. In a different universe,
on a different turtle, we would have blushed.

You pulled my back against your chilled chest
as we rocketed down a log flume
in a painting with a pink sky and baggy trunks
and your heart murmuring on my shoulder.

I pinned a rose to a corkboard in my apartment;
it's dead now, yellow and wilted, but still there,
waiting to turn orange.
I can't see orange, but I suspect
it's similar to fireworks reflected in your green eyes.

I can see the strings. Most people can't.

Fate exists, free will might not–that's for the turtles to
          decide–
but I've always seen the string between our pinkies: Red.
There was no surprise, then, that when our hands met, you
captured me in a perfect cat's cradle.

Only, I can't see color all that well. My cones are small,
and it turns out that red isn't red at all. It's yellow like a
dying rose.

So I sit and wait for turtles to crash.

Shitback

A monkey sits, arm
in my spine as if I'm a
skeletal puppet
twisted by shit-coated hands.

I'm scared of intimacy.

For When You Sweetly Ask If I'm Doing Better

My nails ballet dance against my palms when you ask.
I'm scared of my stutter if I answer, so I obfuscate and say,
I don't actually know anything about quantum physics.

Quarks spin, never choosing direction until observed,
but then when we close our eyes, the universe vanishes.
Object permanence is reserved for toddlers.

We're alone in the cosmos, unaffected, unobserving.
When parallel universes collide, we see ourselves say hello.
I never wave at myself.

Waves and particles are the same and everything is a wave,
but that only applies to light.
We know nothing about light except
how it is captured by blackholes.

Blackholes will destroy everything.
We call this the Big Crunch.
Cosmic death creates the universe.
We call this the Big Bang.
The cyclical theory of
cosmology is the Big Bounce,
but no one believes in that.

The thing is, we don't know what gravity is.
It's why we fall to splatter on sidewalks,
but I don't. At least,
not around you.

I know the graves of my brain,
but I can't answer when you ask about their gravity

because I know nothing about quantum physics.

On a Drive from Bowling Green to Savannah

the trees are dead.
There are leaves and birds still.
But the bark is gray and rotting.
The fashion greenery has leached to autumnal brown.
Dead. Falling. Clinging still, but dead.
The mist of the Smokies rises from the burnt carcasses
that have never tasted fire.
The trees are dead, though I know they are not because
my eyes are the dead ones.

The glasses slumbering in my suitcase
can grant me the courage of colors,
those angry reds, braying browns, and kissing purples
that would fill in the gray spaces,
this drive between homes,
the black and white of dreams and dreary death.
I am floundering in art and love.
I could stop and put them on,
reject the binary, the drive, the death.
But I am lazy and people make fun of rose-colored lenses.
So I drive.

The battery dies an hour before Atlanta.
The gas station lot is empty as I wait for roadside.
The battery is wrong, they tell me two hours later.
The car was sold ineffective and waiting to die.
My parents tell me to not turn it off until I am home.
I cough out half-digested pain pills, red dye
spilling over my fingers.
At another gas station, sky dark, I piss in a fast food cup.

I shiver, warm, as gas fills the humming tank.
There is no explosion.

My tire explodes. It's the back right, where the gas is.
It's as if my car knew I could no longer see the dead trees.
The heavy crunch and rumble of rim on pavement
seemed background chanting, "Hellfire" *Hunchback*,
the angry growl of a voracious animal, mad
to have been fed
under less than ideal conditions. I drove
until a man pulled me over and helped change my tire.

Perhaps it took skill, a malignant unluck,
to add four hours to a ten hour drive.
I slipped into my bed at my parents' house.
Projectors played scenes of the road on my lids.
Tomorrow I must wake and put on my glasses.
I'll go out to the yard and I'll see
if all the trees are dead

or is it only the ones on the drive
from Bowling Green to Savannah?
Tomorrow I must drive again.

On Roman Catholicism

How do you say that butterflies are not beautiful
because when you were young, you heard
butterflies feast on corpses
and when one landed on your arm in the yard
your sister was jealous but you cried
because you thought you were dying
and how now, years past, they whisper
that you, you ugly thing,
will not produce a corpse beautiful enough
to be feasted on by butterflies?

Dear God, It's Me, Jarred

When I was six, the age of princess dress-up
and epic battles between batteries and frayed flip-flops,
news clips played of a tsunami crashed on distant shores,
skeleton children huddled in shattered shelter piles,
and debris danced on green waves.
It was the first time I remember praying.
I folded my hands together and wandered about the house
like Mom did when she was on the phone with her best
        friend,
and I asked you to keep them safe.
I didn't know what death was, not really.

When I was ten, the age of migration and swearing
to stop pissing my pants at school,
a frail boy invited me to play at his Church
in a lock-in where they hid our shoes
before we named the pastor's newborn kittens.
It was my first time in a place of worship.
The evangelizing was likely meant to save my soul.
I teased him about my coming freedom, the migration
out of state where between me and our bullies,
only I would leave him alone. Phones weren't yet the rage.
I didn't know I'd forget his name.

When I was twelve, the age of in-private browsing
and writing low-quality sci-fi novels,
my racist great-grandmother died.
Freemasons preached at her rainy Florida funeral.
It was my first time at the beach.

Butterfly Snuff

I expected more crabs and I was scared of the emerald
      waves,
because, by then, I knew death
and the way it feasts on flesh until nothing remains.
We raced go-karts and ate butter-bathed lobster.
I didn't know fascists and floods would rush to destroy the
      shore.

When I was fourteen, the age of marching band
and belting ballads, off-tune Martina McBride in showers,
comments on news stories of gay marriage
evoked your name when calling me a shit-dicked
      pedophile.
It was the first time I read the Bible.
I never did get past all those begats.
I asked you to forgive whatever sin doomed
my family's name, to wake
and have a choice.
I didn't know they, you were wrong.

At sixteen, the age of activism
and flopping boneless on a stage,
I came out to my friends and my sister
who made an effort not to squirm,
though she defended people who said I was damned.
It was the first time I slept since puberty.
I didn't know how to pray anymore.

At seventeen, the age of cars
and stripping to censored prom music,
the courts struck down marriage bans

and I let myself plan my ungodly dream wedding
where the theme is superheroes and the cake is donuts.
I spent the summer at an academic camp
where air slipped out my brain and inflated my belly.
It felt like I knew nothing, and that tasted of vanilla.

At eighteen, the age of graduation
a stutter bubbled from my lips
and parvo bubbled on my skin –
things children developed, and I was grown.
It was the first time a boy hit on me.
The dorms smelled of lazy masturbation and mold
mixed with a microscopic hint of severe depression.
I started praying again.

At twenty, the age of existentialism
and directing theatre with inhumane amounts of props,
the bare blue mattress-pad of my bed seduced me
with memories of news story tsunamis,
promising tragedy to sweep me in my suicidal urges.
It wasn't the first time I thought about therapy.

At nineteen
I stabbed a Bible to make a prop for a movie
I never made. The knife folded.
Blood leapt from my pinky.
It coated the blade,
and maybe I forgave you,
or maybe realized I never will,
and I said, "Amen."

Synesthesia

Were I to taste the tang of purple
as it trampolines my teeth like saying

Lilac,

would it smell as rain-kicked dirt before
the midsummer storm has broken?

The Sandbox (Because Ringworm)

It's the edges of ends where no one goes,
like the gentle space between a word and a period.
Periods are boulders chasing Indiana
with none of the thrill of being killed.

It's hard to read my putty face, what with
all the ends of words and worlds and hardened clay.
Clay is the skin of natural androids, Pandora Talos,
and my silent mind must mean I'm robotic.

When robots are pressed to beds in that
violent way of men who fuck,
they cannot cry and wonder
what this means for love.

When men start to fall in love, I take
them to the nearest park
and sit by the sandbox no one plays in
because of ringworm.

Dream Boy Demise

At first, I fell into a cankerous chasm
overrun with festering cancer boils
bursting with carnivorous butterflies.

Then it was falling through teeth and worlds,
too many to count, though the Muppets would try
with their scatted words and hands in my back.

I landed in a tennis match with an officer
who stalked up to the net after I lobbed a serve,
shotgun blasting away my lungs.

Then came the drownings and stabbings,
both all at once, on the beach, swept away,
fetching blankets from the car for flooding sidewalks.

Finally came the shootings, mass and in public,
at university and malls, repeating,
where no matter my choices, I lost my

I see him. He has a new lover. He has a new fat.
His dog bounds up onto my legs. *Hello, loaf.*
His arms wrap around me. I smell him. He breaks up with
        me again.

Dreams have a habit of bleeding.
Walking to my car, my ribs explode out my back and I
become that most monstrous of things: a waking butterfly.

Inception, Conception

My dream self often floats on his stomach
two feet off the ground, one of the super-powered,
of sorts, at least.

After watching years of cinema where the props
and sets are clearly fake, it is now hard to
tell when rocks are real.

A Saran-wrapped snow puts filters on my eyes.
I step off the parking garage roof and wonder
when I'll start to float.

The amniotic sack holds me suspended
like the political campaign I'd have lost in another life,
one where I'm shot in the chest at 43.

The Thunder of the Velvet Ficus

booms when it tips over the linoleum of the kitchen
floor at some metaphorically important time of the early
     morning
that we should call night.

The echo tears as a gunshot in the Alley Imaginary
outside my college apartment where hours
in buried electric libraries built an illusion of safety.

It rumbles against the floor, a phone buzzing
with a text from my beloved,
all sudden excitement before crashing out.

The caesura after summons a creature in my closet,
hung by his neck among the clothes
and I will never learn if you kiss the piece kept to the left of
     your bed.

And I am still in love.
And I am still in bed.

And the thunder of the velvet ficus booms.
And I sob in the ache of the encore.

720 Patton Way

I heard the screams of a dying man
feet outside my apartment on Patton Way
where police tape blanket-stretched over my car
and I sat still in my bed

The pops burst in three rips that stripped
the wax from my ears and shook
the walls as bombs ballooned over Bowling Green
and I sat still in my bed

The screams were whales,
a breech and a spray of blood from blue blow holes
diving to the waves of a getaway car
and I sat still in my bed

The tires squealed in a warning plea
from the manic Fates to Eurydice that the road to hell
had sparkles, shattered windshields, and innard-pinks
and I sat still in my bed

A woman elephant-rampaged through the yard
with barbed words flying off her tongue
garbled and throaty, "My Brother!"
and I sat still in my bed

The police came taking statements door to door,
said the screaming dying man was dead,
and I said *I heard three shots*, they left,
and I sat still in my bed

and I sat still in my bed.

Afterimage

It's the relativity of time that curses us
and tantalizes the mind with the idea of travel.
I would gank baby Hitler, says the made-up fuck boy
who answers when asked about changing the past.

It's Garth Brooks who croons that, could he go
to before the pain, he wouldn't change a thing lest he
miss that singularly fantastic dance
entangled on your bed with my nose in your neck.

The trauma of being born cleaved my mind in half.
I live seconds in the future and fire warning flares,
yet my body only responds to my
afterimage.

So when you said *Goodbye* and *Let's be friends*,
as the ocean's tide rose to swallow
my shivering hips, I tried to say *Okay*,
but it came out

I love you.

Upon Hearing "Something" by the Beatles on the Radio Instead of Your Couch, Cranberry Vodka Drunk

Records
spin on the court
gavel point sentences
handed down from the radio
static.

Ars Corpus

Men don't have stretchmarks, my poetry professor
in undergrad said during a workshop session
when I did lines on the purple stretches over my sides and
        ass.

After graduation, 2020, my name killing thousands,
I got into my first relationship with a coward
who tuned and fixed me as a broken guitar, strung along.

In bed, he touched the angry colors that climbed my hip.
What happened? he asked in horrified tones and insisted it
        was a wound.
I kissed the acne scars on his back. I always did the kissing.

I did lines with him in his kitchen. *I love you*, first time
        mutters
in those days when he insisted I was his while sneaking
me inside the home that he owned to hide from friends I
        already knew.

I have prosecuted a bad case against myself.
The only evidence he was embarrassed of me is
        non-conclusive.
Like all detectives, I nearly drank myself to death in its
        pursuit.

What would he think now when more marks coat my skin?
Actors go insane because we have to see ourselves on
        screen.
I am but a curling chin and growing gut.

Butterfly Snuff

It is immoral to talk to myself in the ways I do.
My self-deprication leads to scolding by my friends.
The new marks ripple and itch beneath the hair of my
        stomach.

The internet says it is bigoted to hate yourself
which is convenient in that it gives me another reason
to increase the cruel thoughts I've always shot into my
        stomach.

I consider making amateur porn. Let the thirsty gays
            connect
the thousands of brown dots across my flesh. I only
            recently
learned that moles are not red. The world of true color is
        depressing.

My ass has driven men wild. It won an award in college.
Cute say the men who want to abuse me, to fuck
my face into a spit and cum-coated mess.

Someone once ran his hands over my arms in the middle
of a movie and muttered occasionally about his love for my
        Italian fur.
There is love to be found in my body. For it.

I haven't snorted snow since my ex dashed my heart on
        Savannah cobblestone.
Our last conversation was in a gas station parking lot.
Even then, he never said what he liked about me.

One day my body will be only the stretch, pulled and
        wrinkled,
itching and discolored, growing, consuming, contagious
        COVID corona.
I wish to be the bite-size of an ant.

The middle knuckle on my left hand can twitch in a fist.
That's gross, people gasp as they pull away. And finally I
        get to say,
I know.

The Midnight Butterfly

Drifting through the stories of the Victorian
home on Windsor and Park as I pad down the halls
and faucet-fall blood from my nose, I see
the shadow of the midnight butterfly.

What difference lies in imagination and hallucination?
I once played epics starring AA batteries and sneakers.
Sat in College Lit 200, fall 2016, I lose days
drifting through the stories of the Victorian.

A cold breeze and a creek on the floor–I woke, young,
my shirt wet and colored, my parents shouting downstairs,
I watch the eyeless, hatted man float over the rails of my
home on Windsor and Park as I pad down the halls.

Snow, dust, angel, coke–who gives a shit what you call it?
It burns through the curled fiver.
I dance over my boyfriend's floor
and faucet-fall blood from my nose.

Fluoxetine stays my fault-line lungs from tearing
my hands, deep purple geodes swallowed in the dawn.
I lay in bed, dry-tongued, hard-nosed, chasing after
the shadow of the midnight butterfly.

Acknowledgements

Some of the poems in this collection have been previously published. I extend my sincere gratitude to those publishers and all who have read my work.

"Fishbowl" was originally published in *Zephyrus* by Western Kentucky University in 2020

"The Consequences of Being Colorblind" was originally published in *Zephyrus* by Western Kentucky University in 2020

"Oscar Isaac Wore a Hat" was originally published by FreezeRay Poetry in issue #19.

About the Author

 Jarred Corona is a poet, playwright, author, actor, saxophonist, and musical theatre composer from Savannah, GA. He's a graduate of Western Kentucky University. His plays and musicals can be found on the New Play Exchange. He often ruminates on death, time, philosophy, horror, and violence.